Adult Coloring Book

Butterflies and Flowers

Relax with this Calming, Stress Managment, Butterflies and Flowers Coloring Book for Adults

Grahame David Garlick

www.southshorepublications.com

Copyright © 2015 SouthShore Publications

ISBN-13: 978-1518895678

ISBN-10: 1518895670

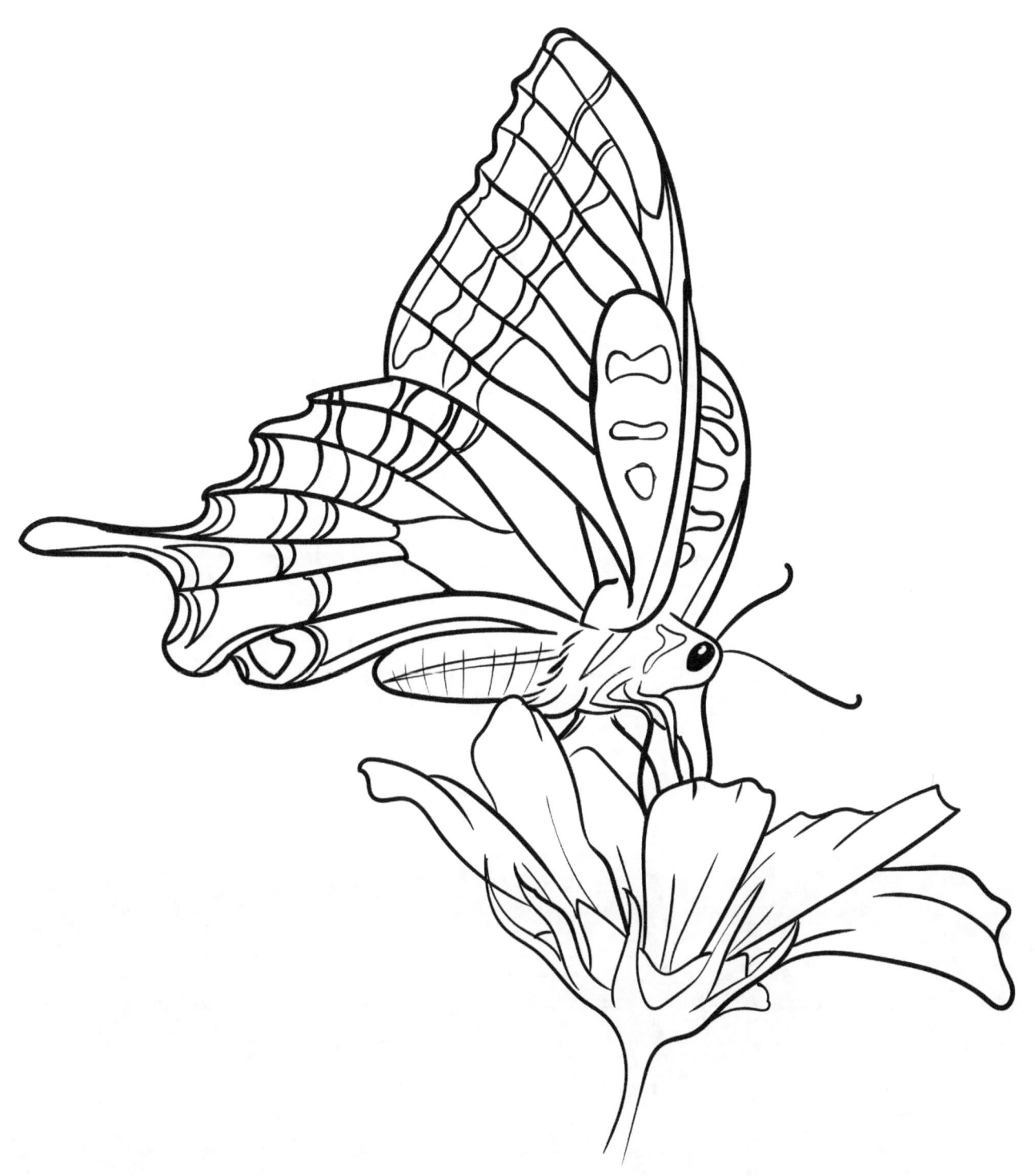

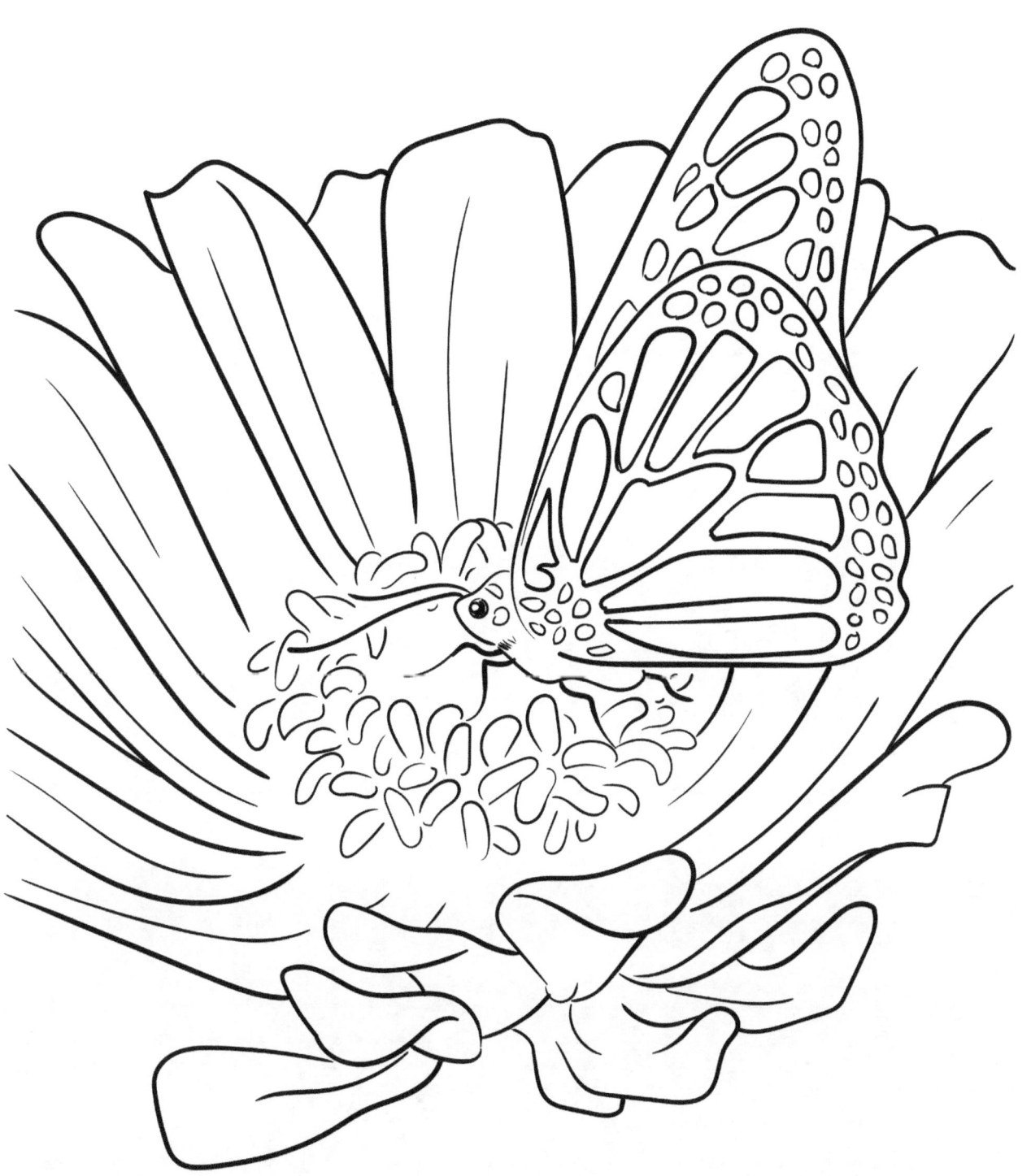

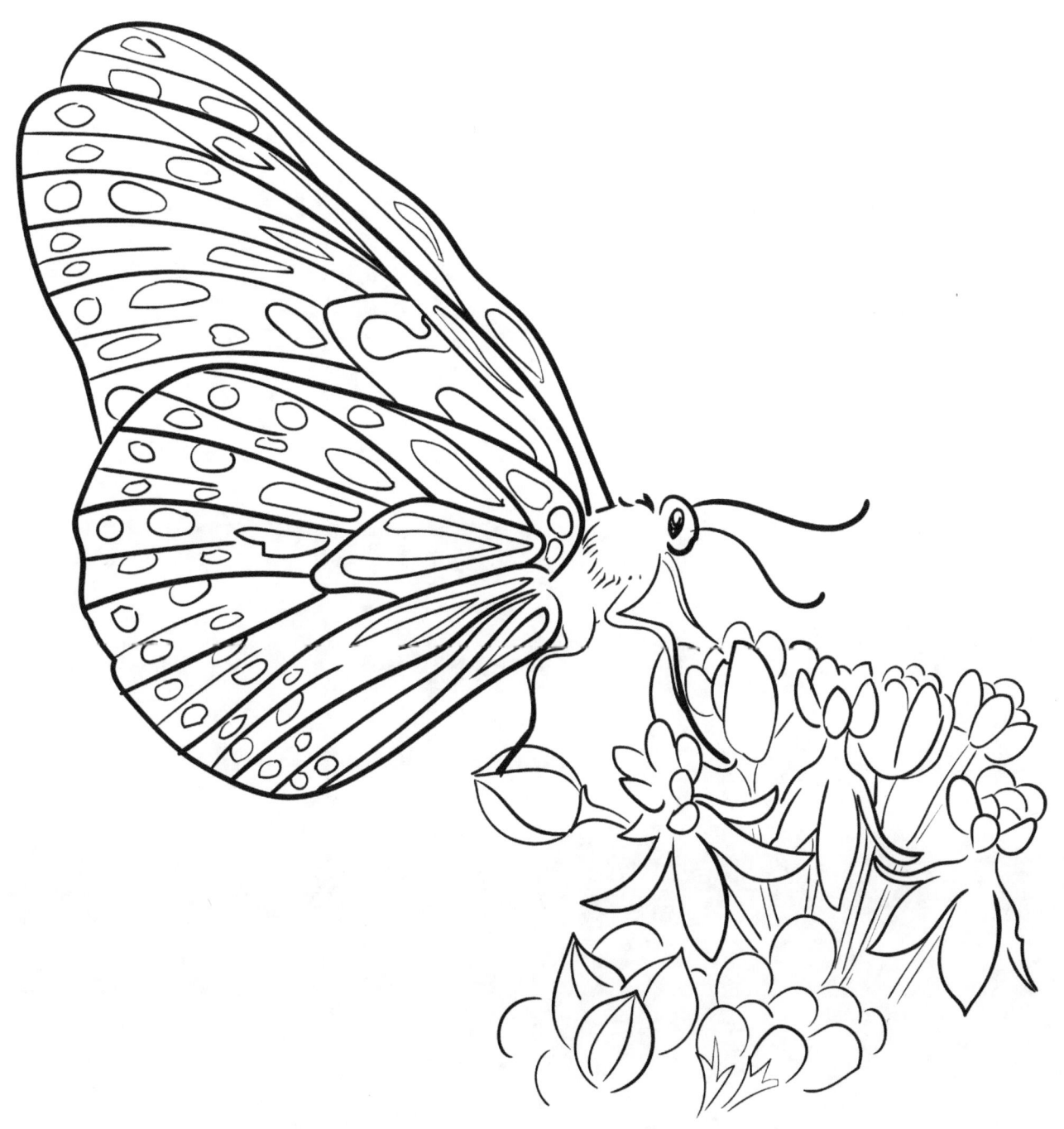

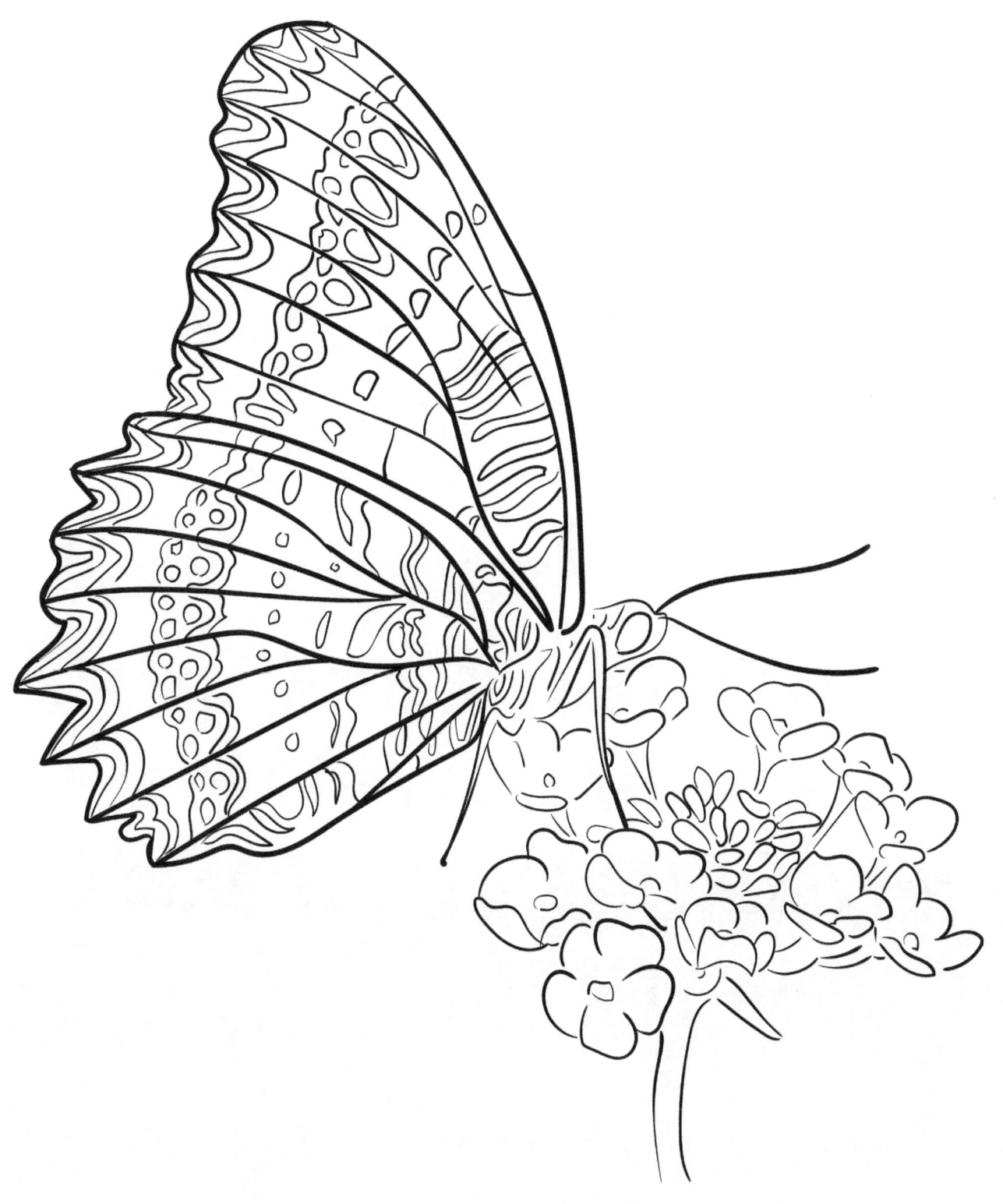

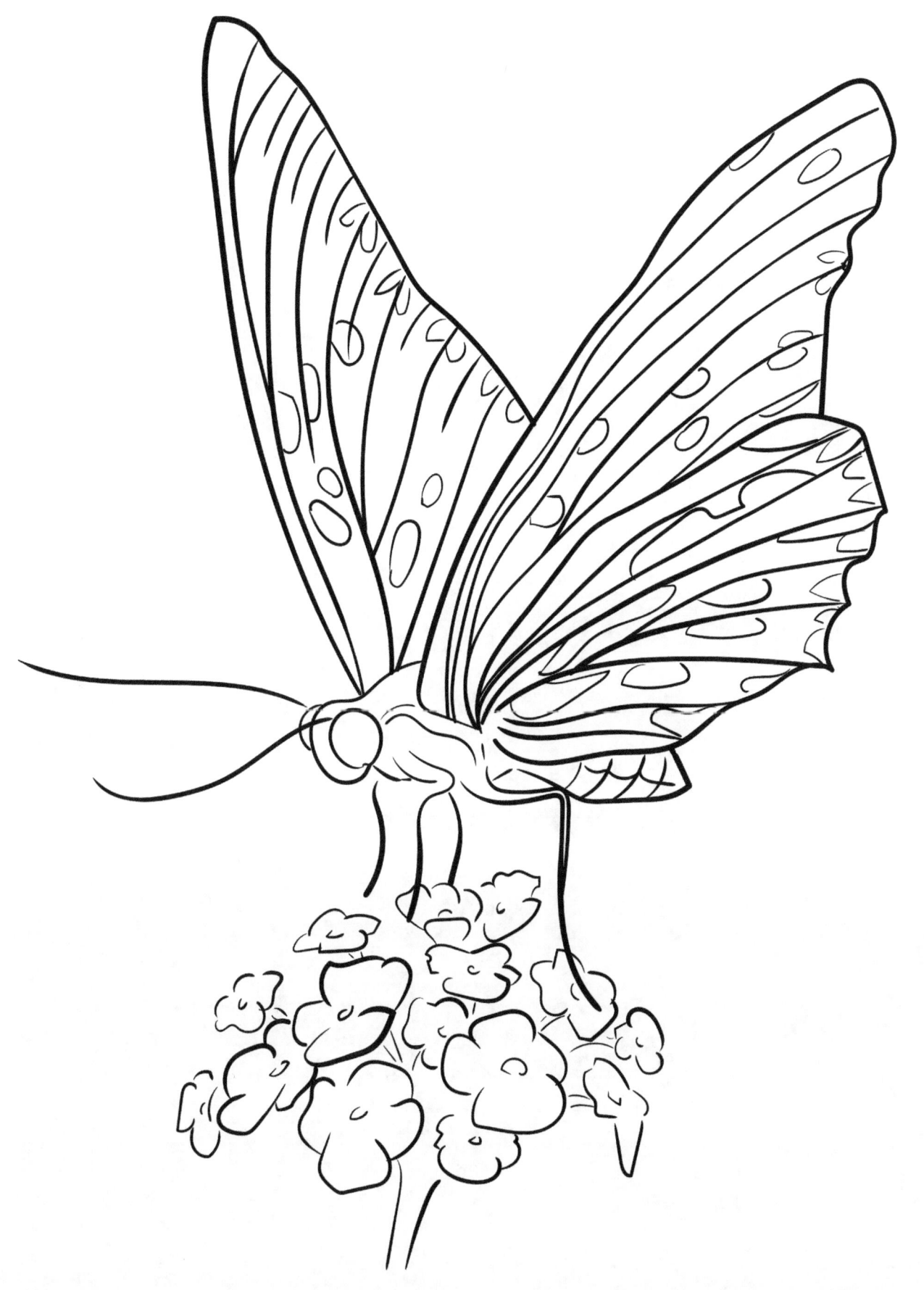

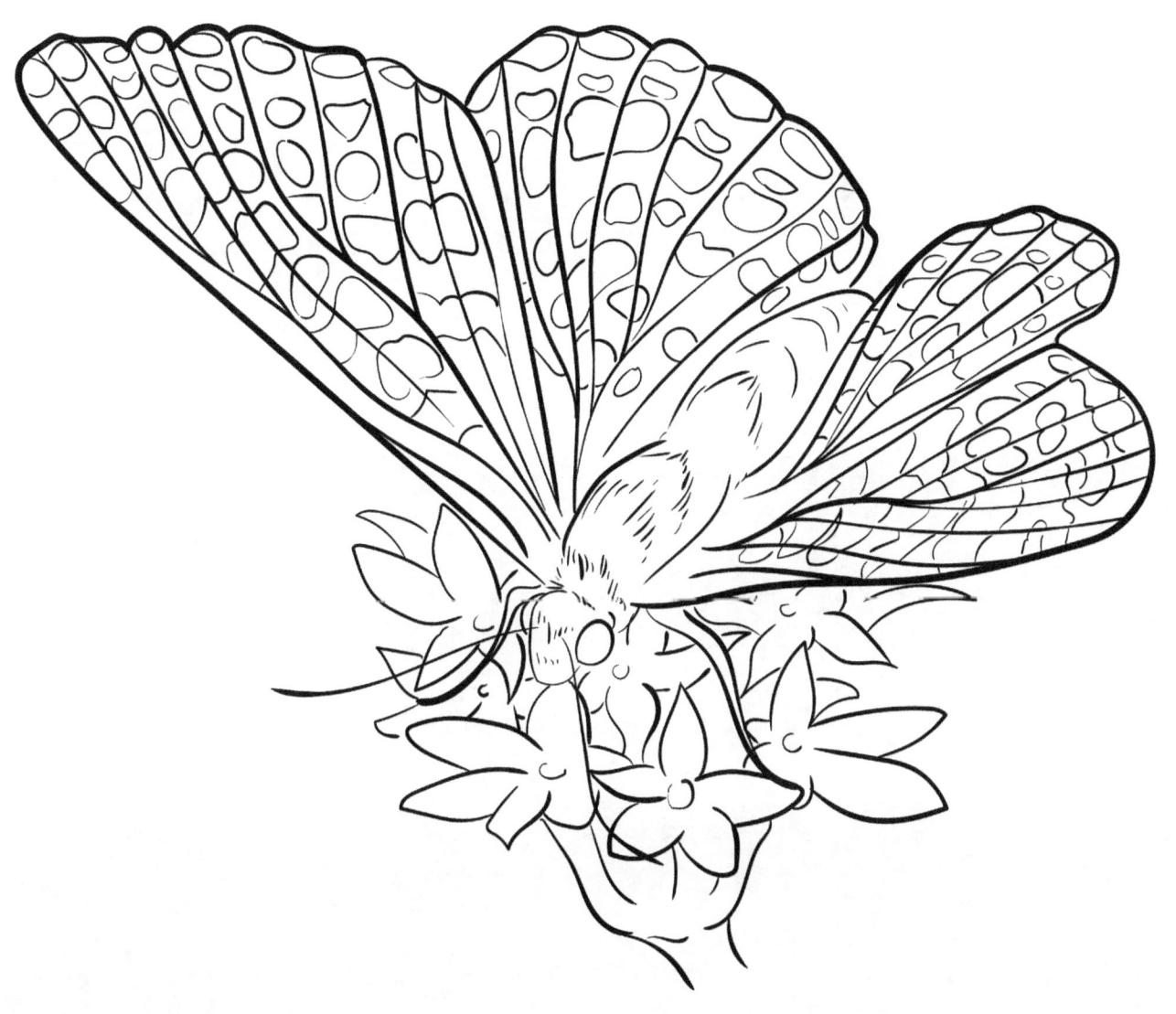

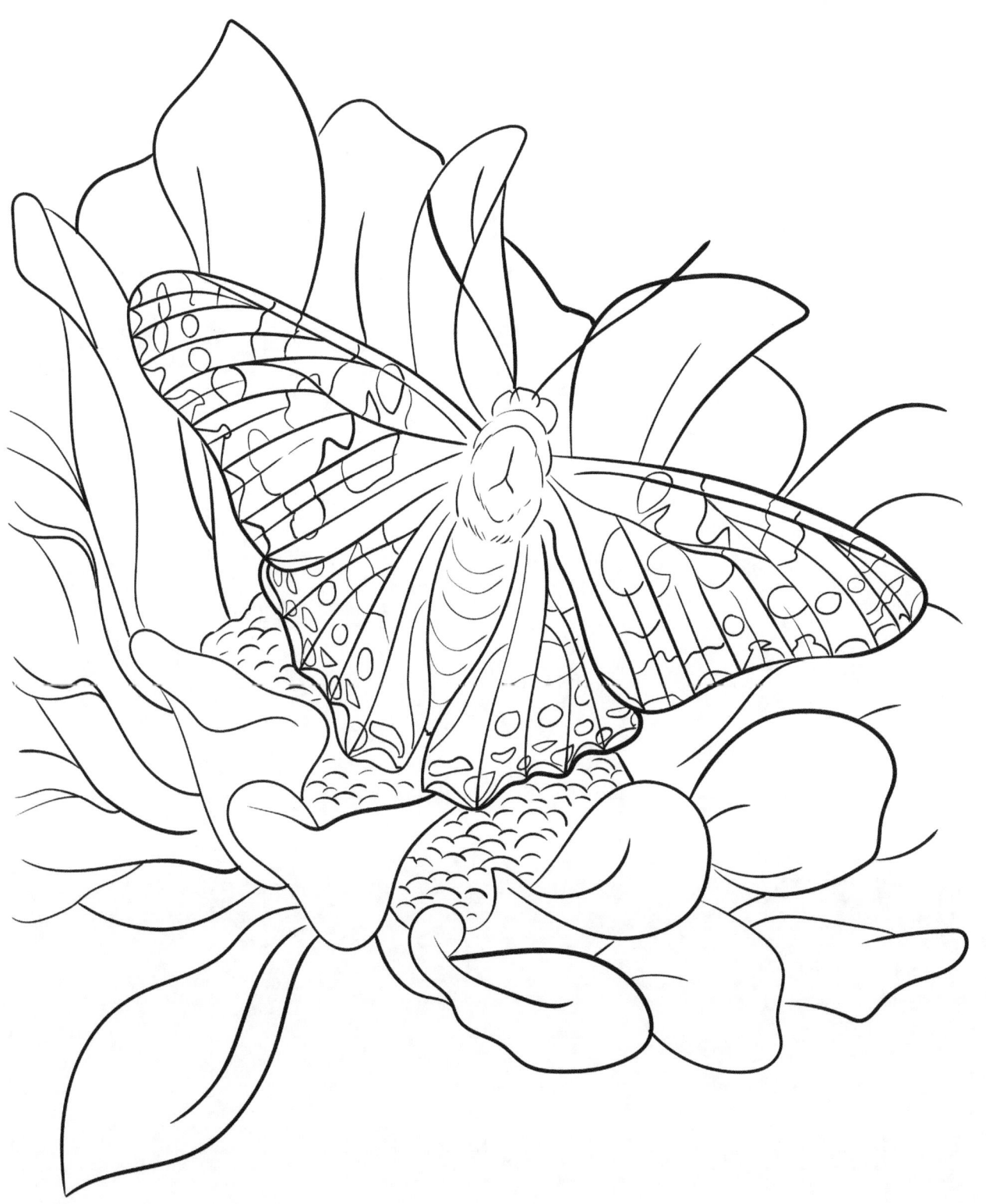

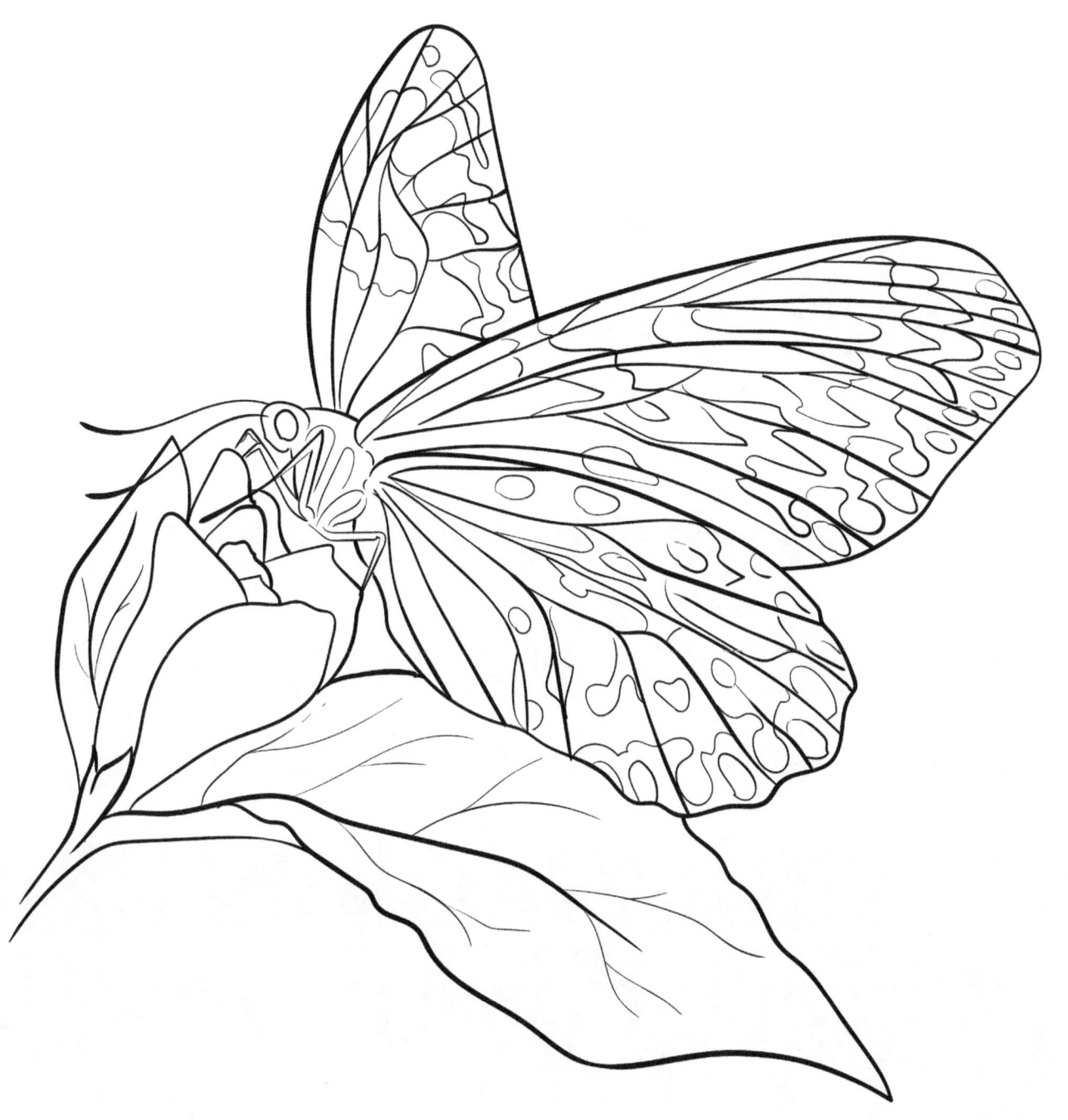

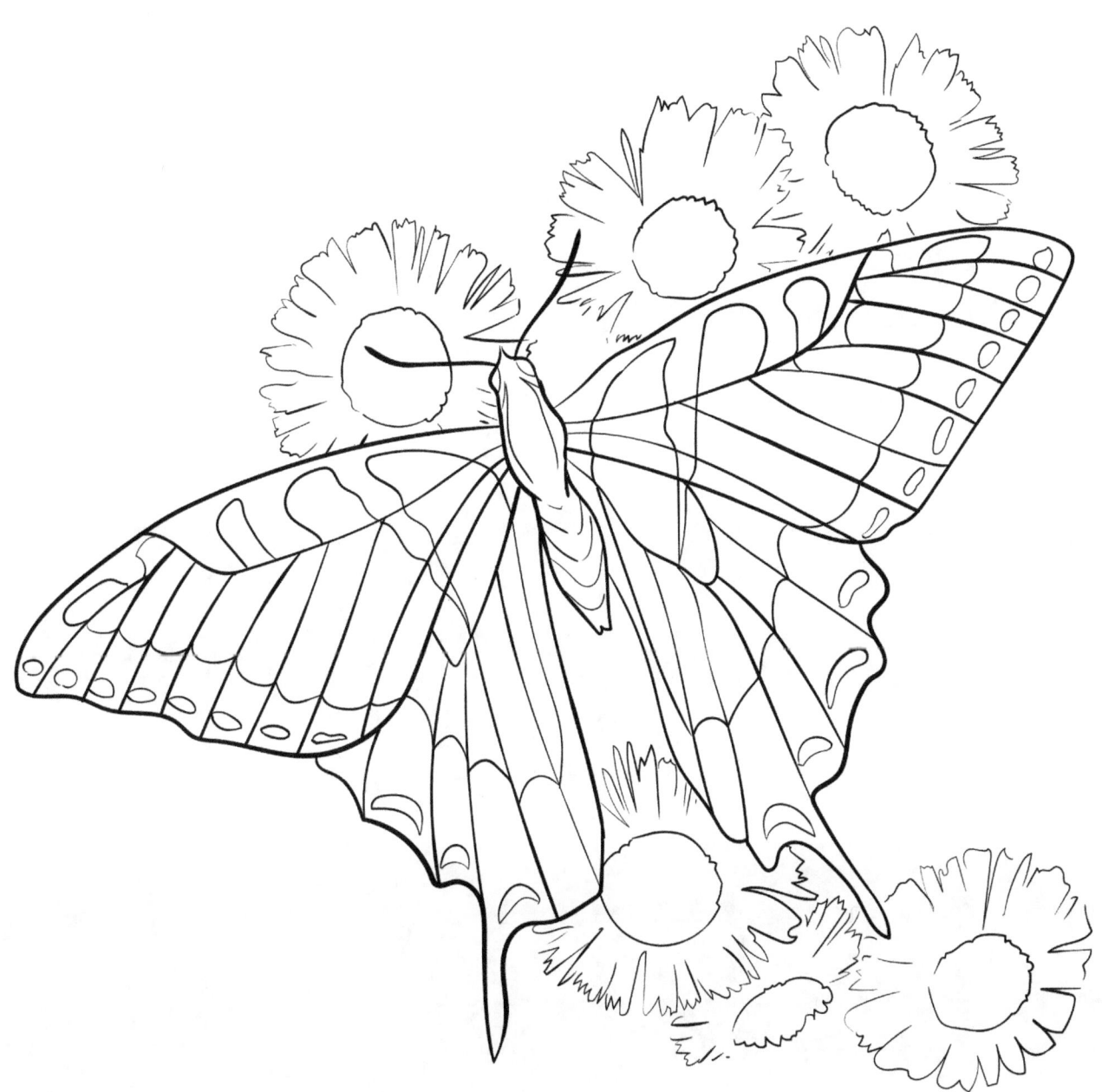

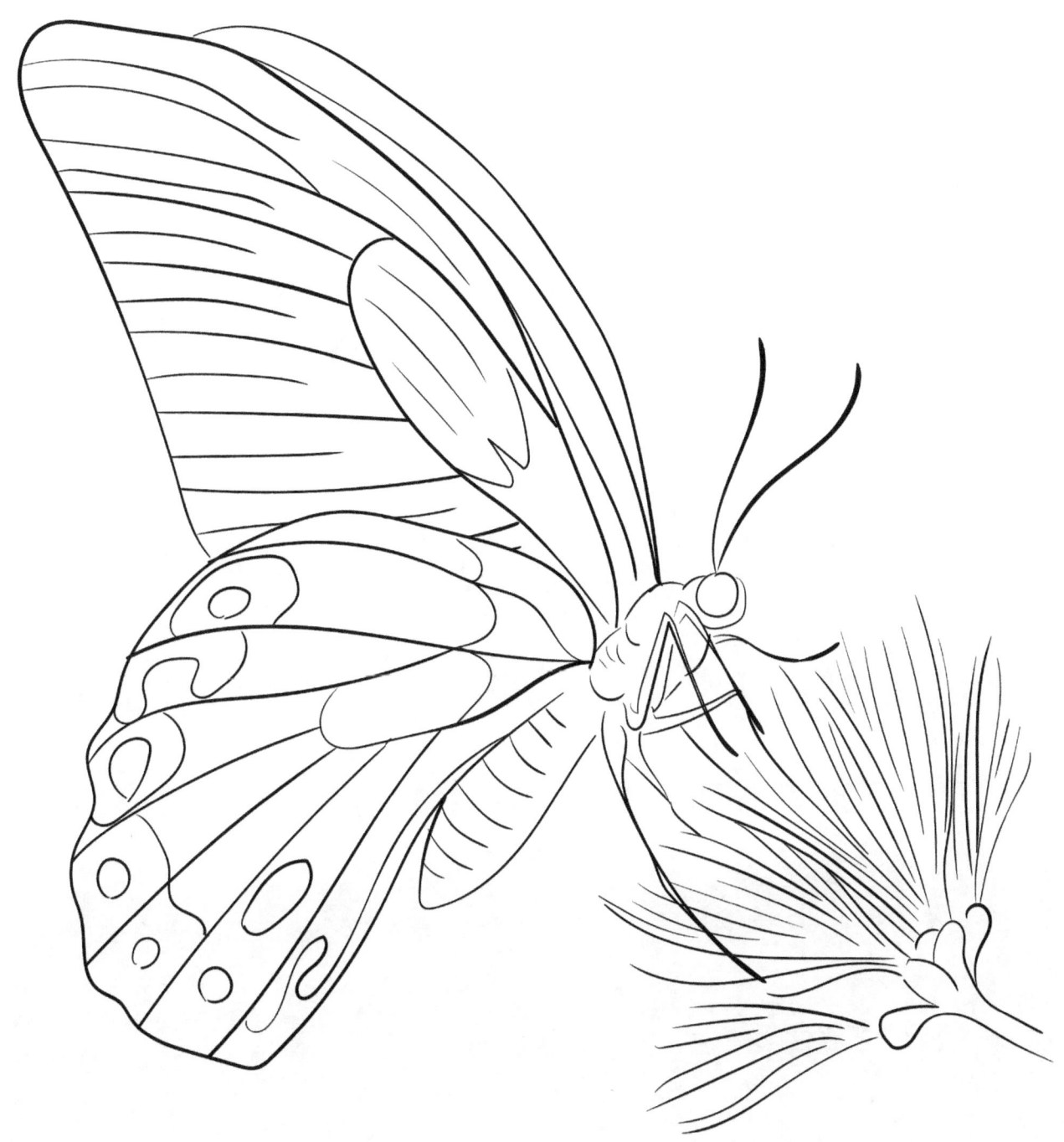

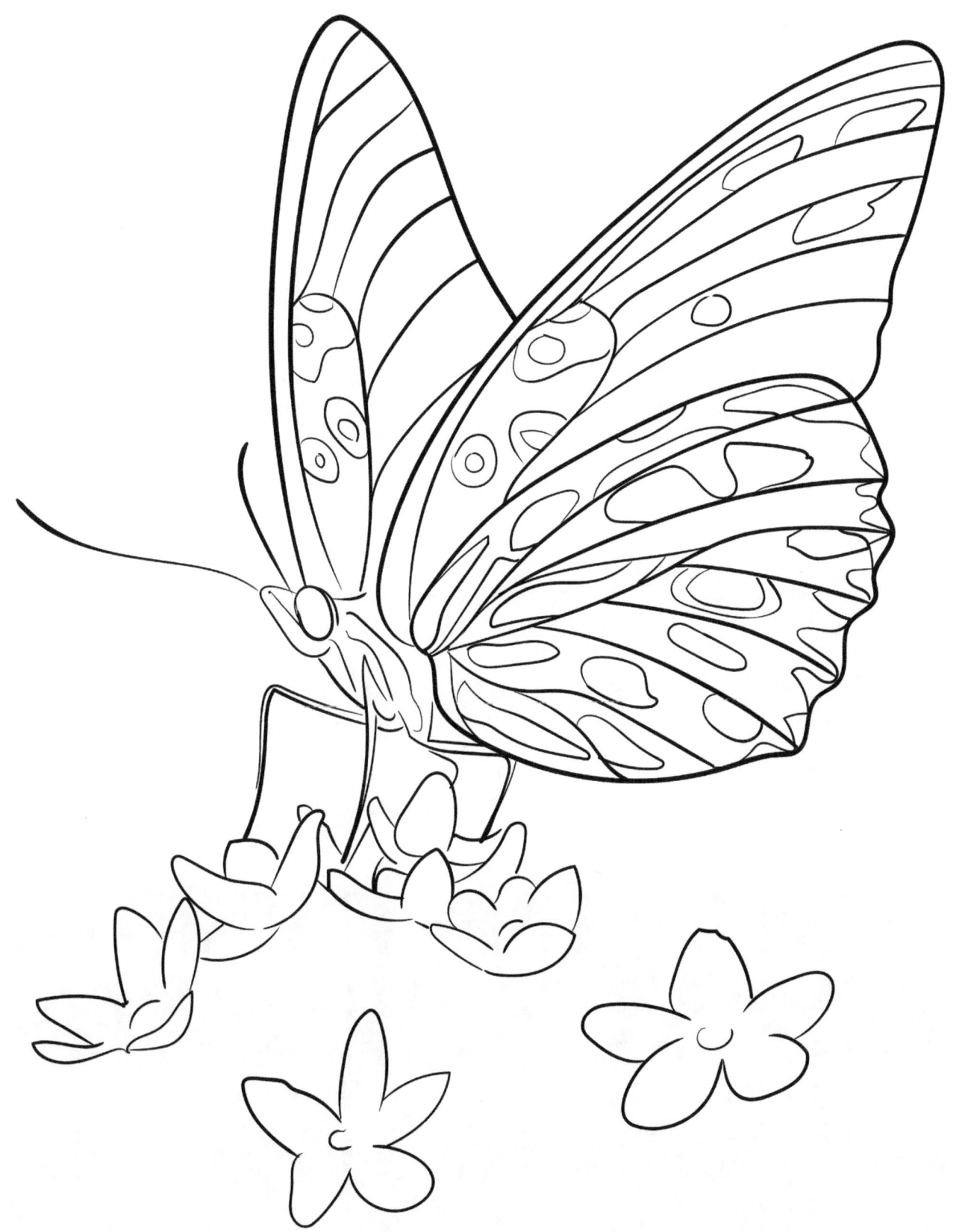

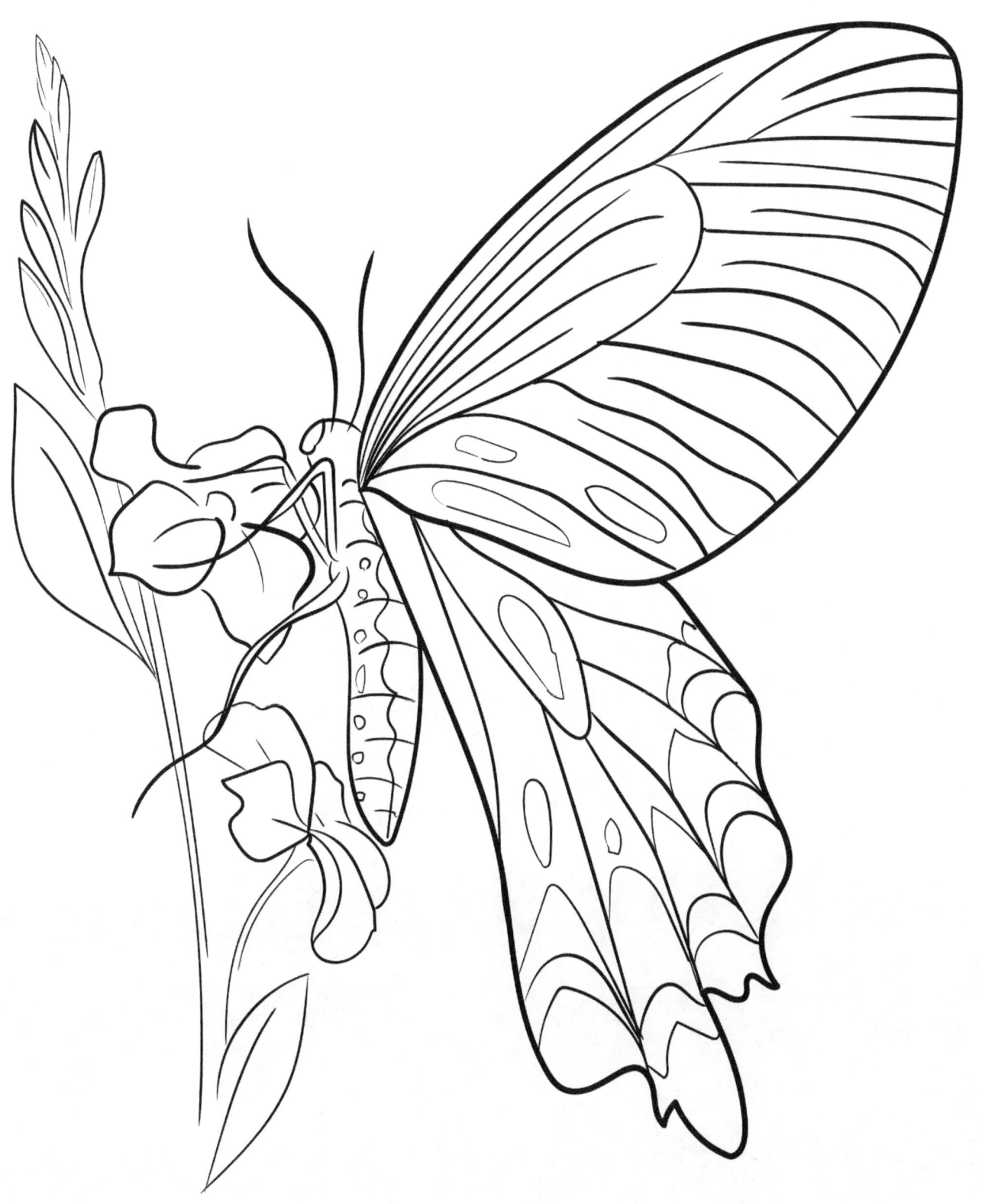

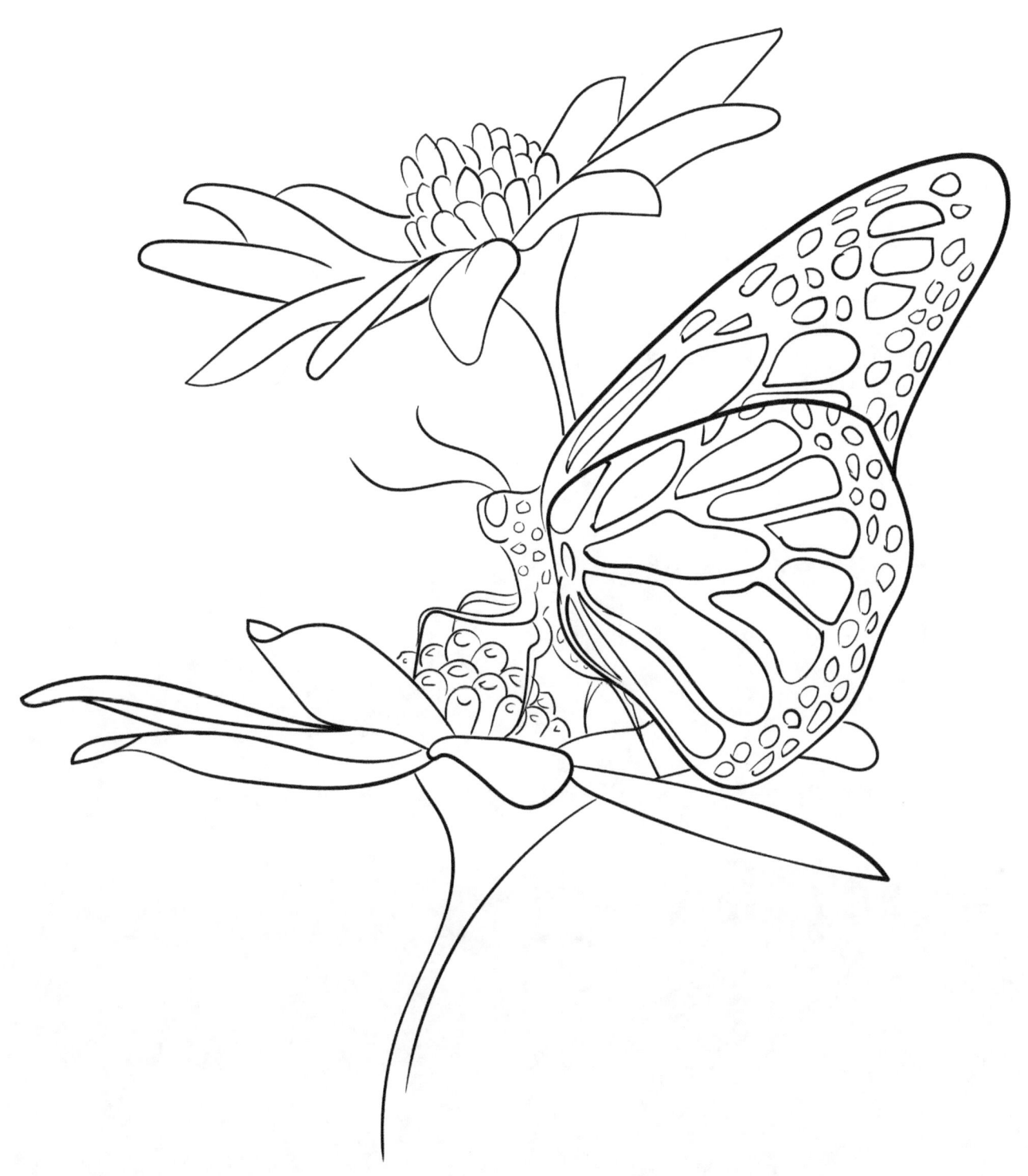

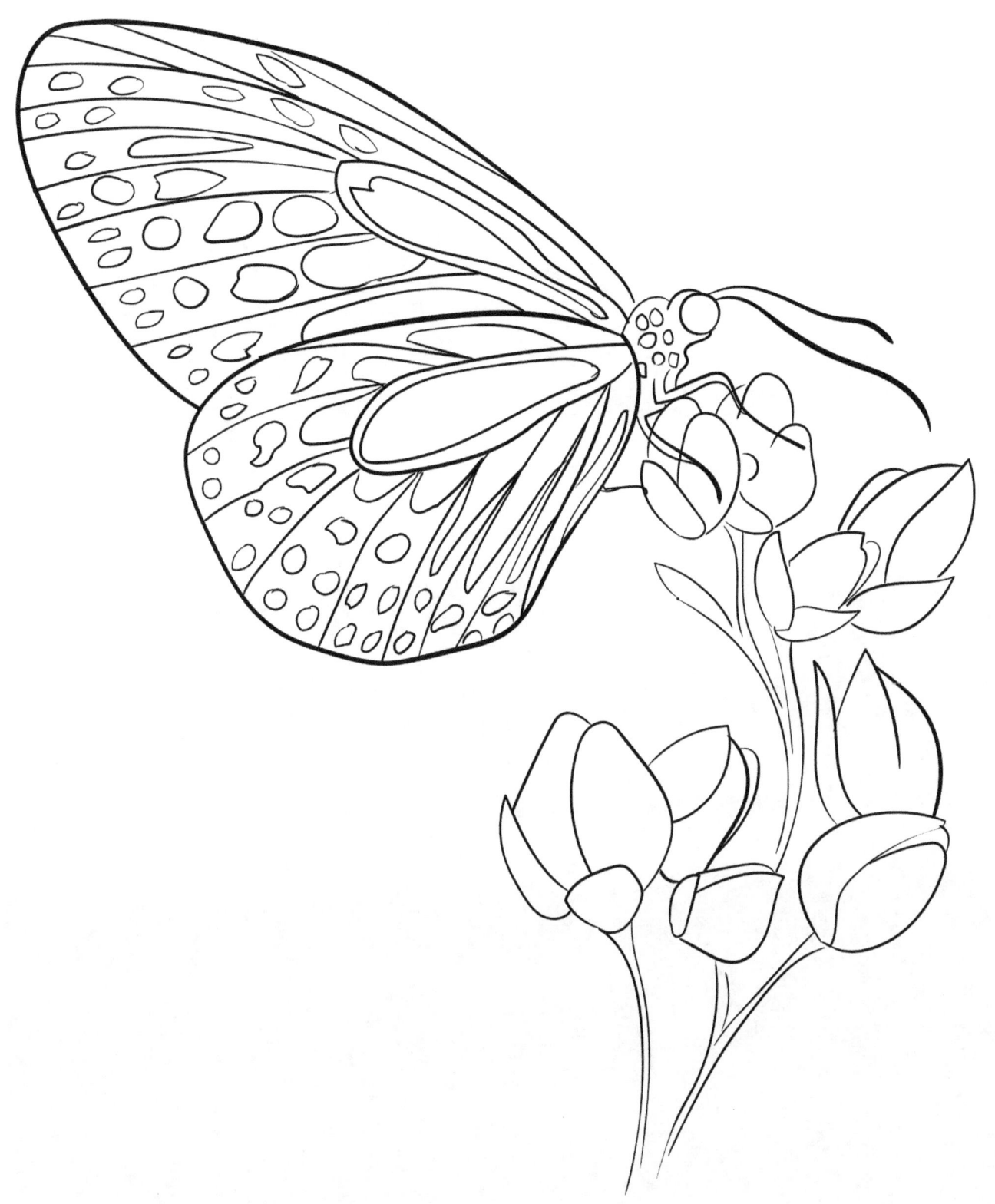

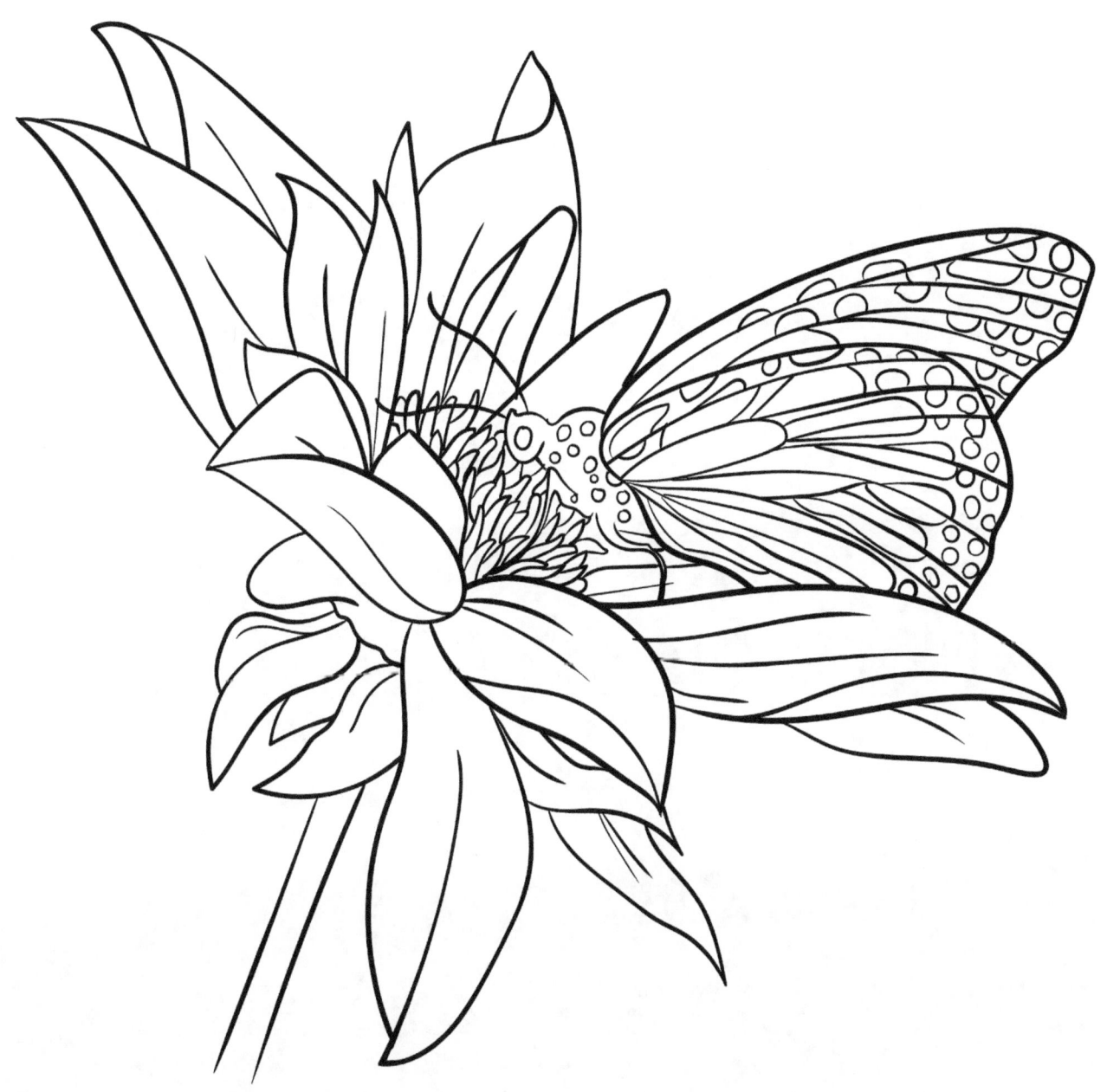

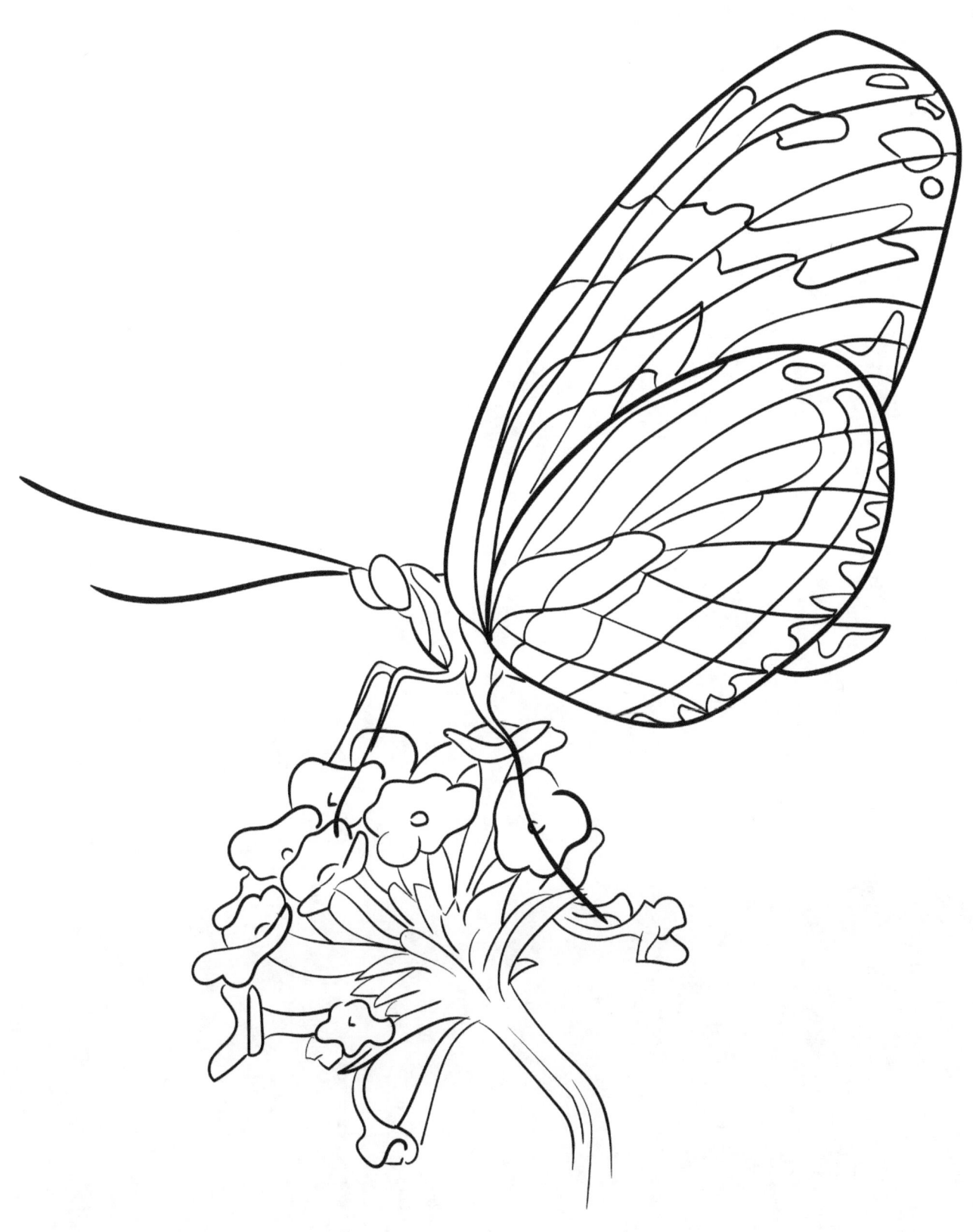

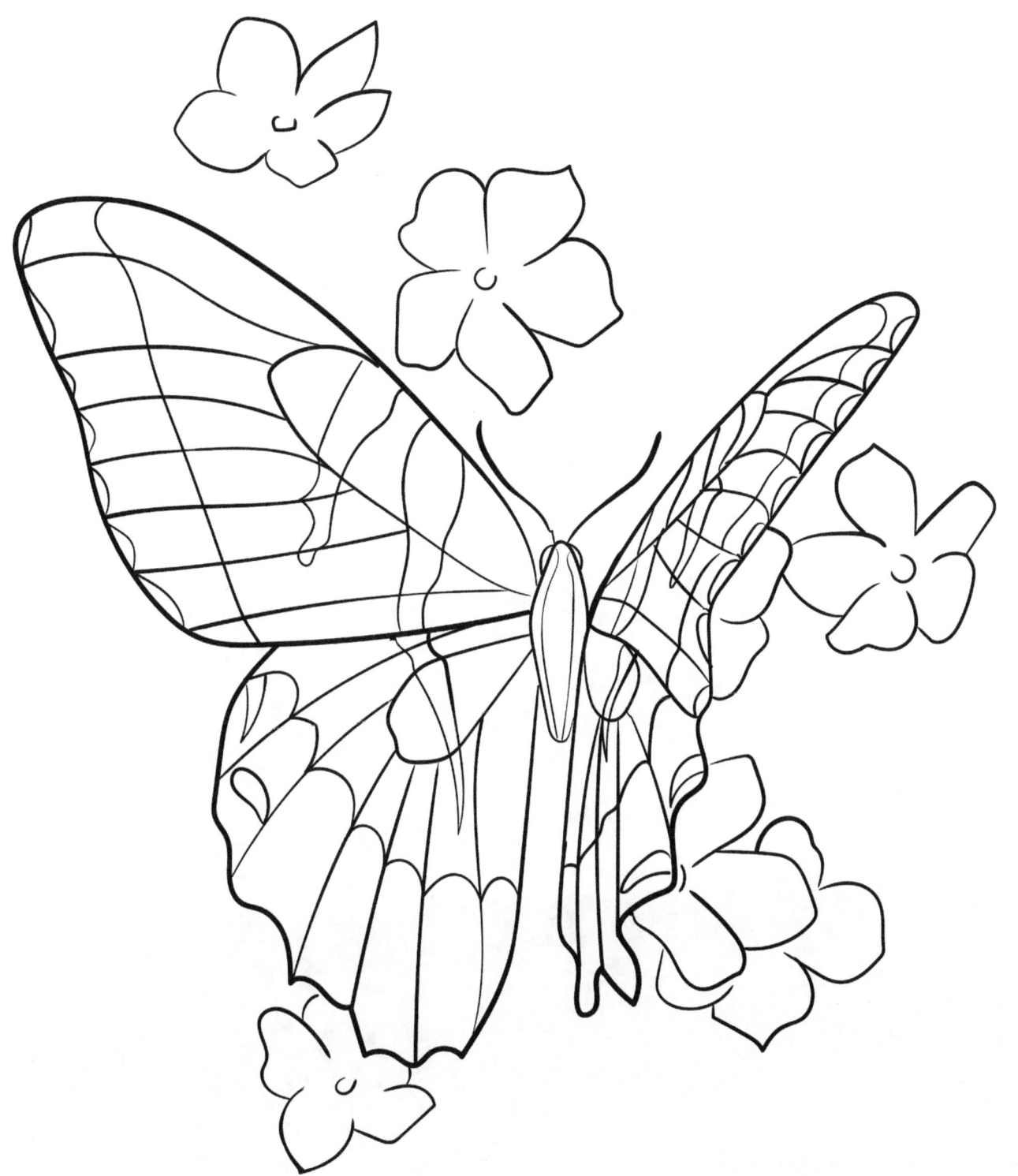

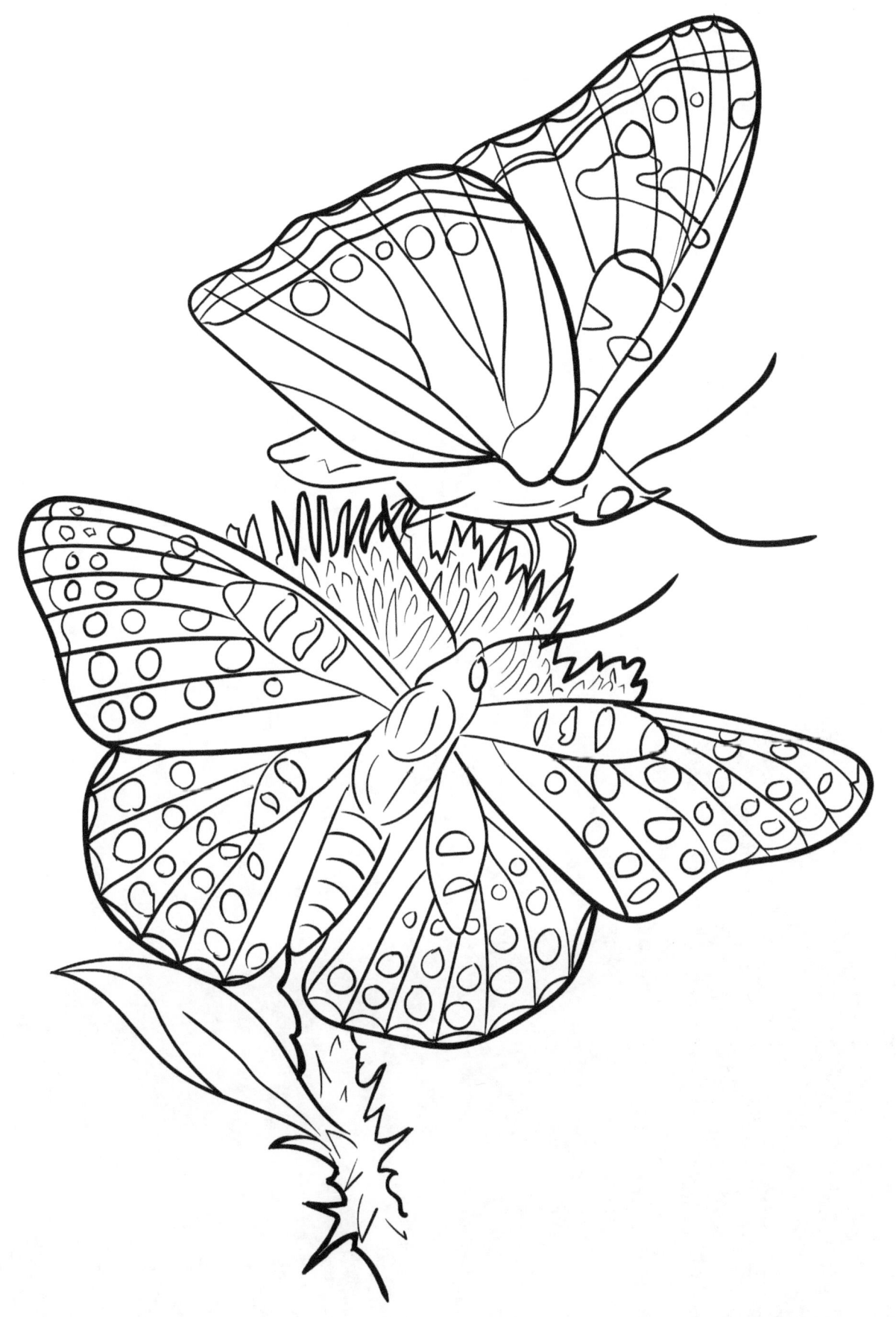

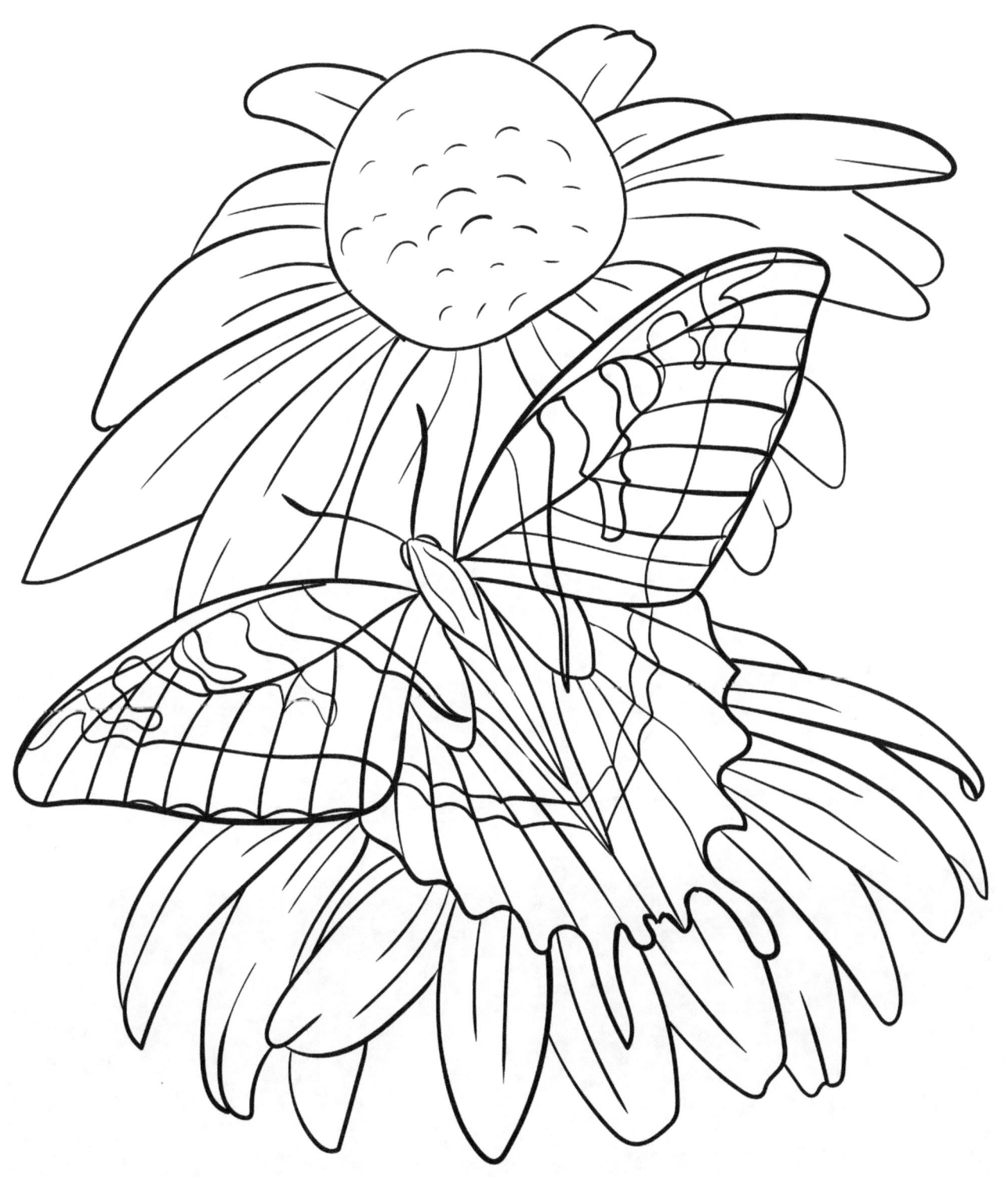

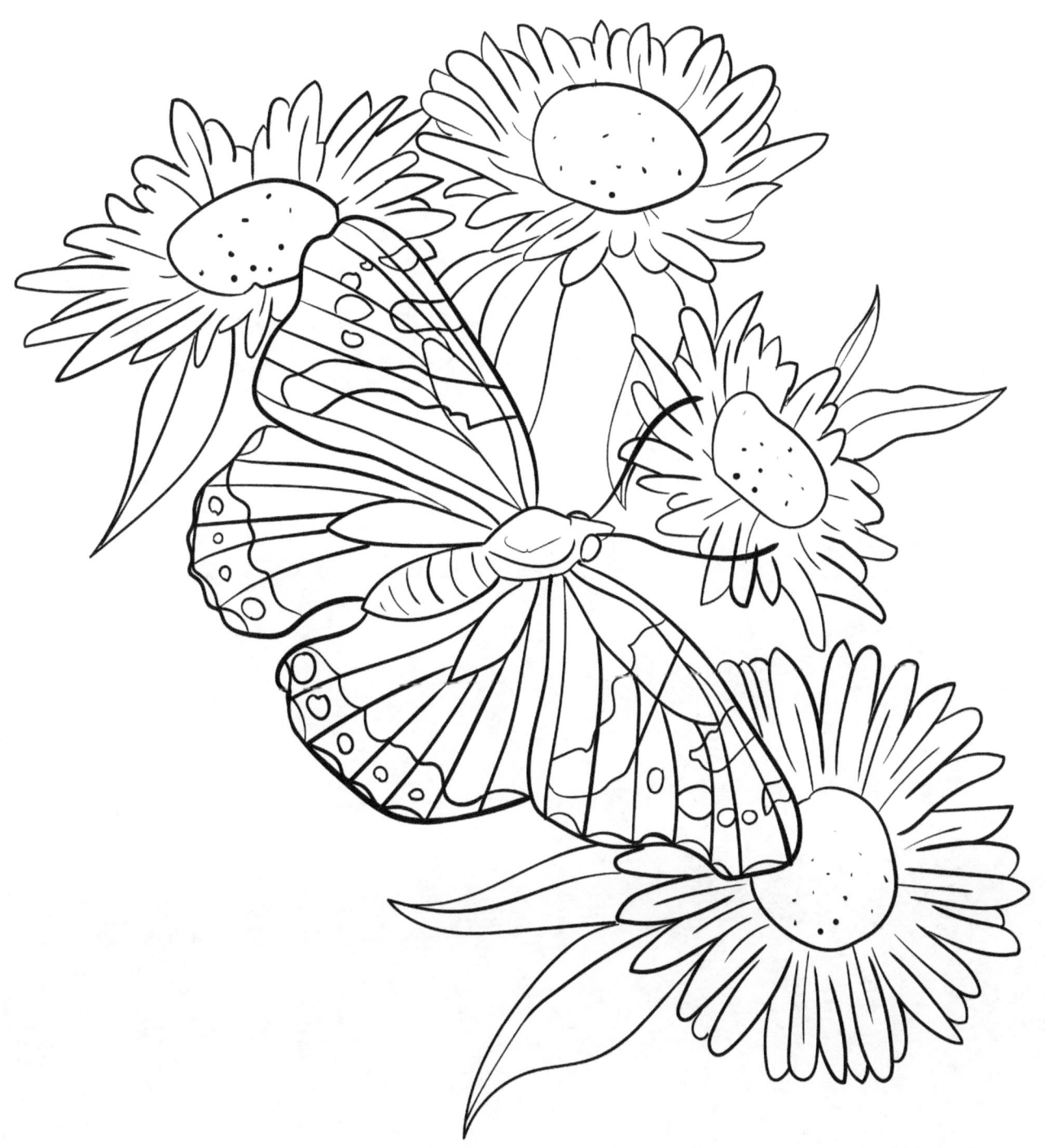